LOTS OF DO___

baby quilts

These playful quilts celebrate the simple shape that makes the world go 'round. Pieced and appliquéd circles and a sprinkling of polka-dots make them fun!

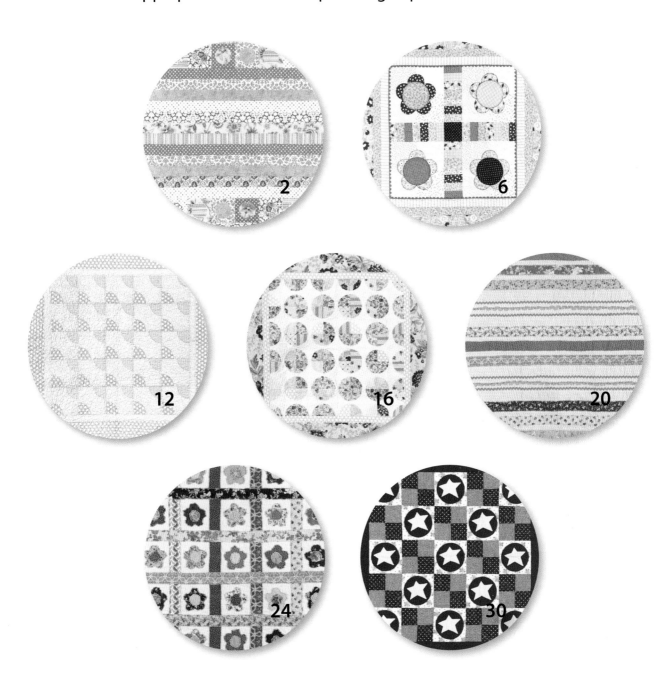

LEISURE ARTS, INC. • Maumelle, Arkansas

DOTS & STRIPES

Finished Size: 37" x 38" (94 cm x 97 cm)

SHOPPING LIST

Yardage is based on 43"/44" (109 cm/112 cm) wide fabric with a usable width of 40" (102 cm).

☐ Jelly Roll* with at least 14 **strips**

☐ Charm Pack* with at least 32 **squares**

☐ $1/2$ yd (46 cm) of fabric for binding

☐ $2^5/_8$ yds (2.4 m) of fabric for backing

You will also need:

☐ 45" x 46" (114 cm x 117 cm) piece of batting

☐ Paper-backed fusible web

☐ Stabilizer

***OR** $1^3/_4$ yds (1.6 m) **total** of assorted print fabrics. Jelly Rolls are assortments of $2^1/_2$" wide strips. Charm Packs are assortments of 5" x 5" squares.*

CUTTING THE PIECES

*Follow **Rotary Cutting**, page 36, to cut fabric. Cut all strips from the selvage-to-selvage width of the fabric. All measurements include 1/4" seam allowances.*

From assorted print fabrics:

- Cut 14 **strips** 2¹/₂" wide if not using Jelly Roll.
- Cut 16 **squares** 5" x 5" if not using Charm Pack.

From fabric for binding:

- Cut 5 **binding strips** 2¹/₂" wide.

CUTTING THE APPLIQUÉS

*Follow **Preparing Fusible Appliqué Pieces**, page 37, and use circle pattern, page 5, to cut appliqués.*

From Charm Pack or assorted print fabrics:

- Cut 16 **circles**.

MAKING THE APPLIQUÉD BLOCKS

*Follow **Machine Blanket Stitch Appliqué**, page 38, to make Blocks.*

1. Center and fuse 1 **circle** to each **square**. Blanket Stitch appliqué circles to make 16 Appliquéd Blocks.

Appliquéd Block (make 16)

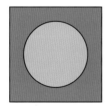

ASSEMBLING THE QUILT TOP

*Follow **Piecing** and **Pressing**, page 37, to assemble quilt top. Refer to Quilt Top Diagram for placement. Use 1/4" seam allowances throughout.*

1. Matching long edges, sew 12 **strips** together to make **Quilt Top Center**. *Tip: Sew every other seam in the opposite direction.* Trim Quilt Top Center to 36¹/₂" wide.
2. Sew 8 Appliquéd Blocks together to make **inner border**. Make 2 inner borders.
3. Trim 2 strips to 36¹/₂" long for **outer borders**.
4. Matching centers and corners, sew inner borders to Quilt Top Center. In the same manner, sew outer borders to quilt top.

COMPLETING THE QUILT

1. Follow **Quilting**, page 40, to mark, layer, and quilt as desired. Our quilt is machine quilted with meandering quilting in the strips. A swirl is quilted in each circle, and each circle and square is quilted in the ditch.
2. Follow **Making a Hanging Sleeve**, page 42, if a hanging sleeve is desired.
3. Follow **Making Straight Grain Binding**, page 44, and use **binding strips** to make binding. Follow **Attaching Binding with Mitered Corners**, page 44, to bind quilt.

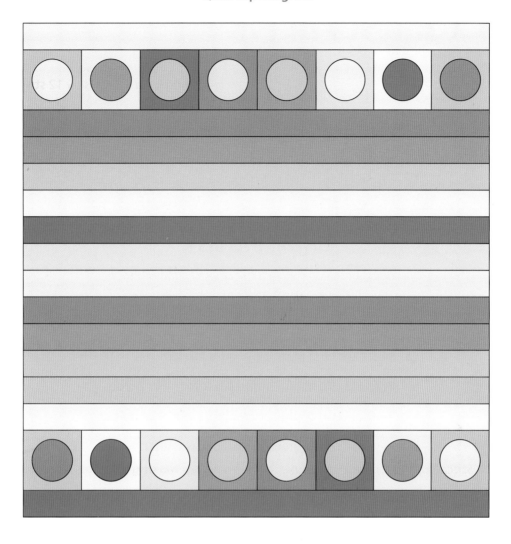

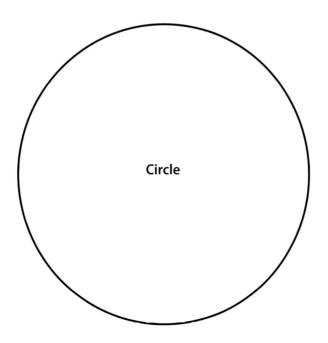

Circle

BLOSSOMS

Finished Size: 36½" x 36½" (93 cm x 93 cm)
Finished Block Size: 10½" x 10½" (27 cm x 27 cm)

SHOPPING LIST

Yardage is based on 43"/44" (109 cm/112 cm) wide fabric with a usable width of 40" (102 cm).

☐ 4 Fat Quarters* of light print fabrics

☐ 8 Fat Quarters* of medium print fabrics

☐ ¼ yd (23 cm) of blue stripe fabric for inner border

☐ ¼ yd (23 cm) of pink print fabric for middle border

☐ ⅜ yd (34 cm) of green print fabric for outer border

☐ ½ yd (46 cm) of fabric for binding

☐ 2½ yds (2.3 m) of fabric for backing

You will also need:

☐ 44" x 44" (112 cm x 112 cm) piece of batting

☐ 3 yds (2.7 m) of ½" (13 mm) wide blue rickrack

☐ Paper-backed fusible web

☐ Stabilizer

***OR** ⅝ yd (57 cm) **total** of assorted light print fabrics and ¾ yd (69 cm) **total** of assorted medium print fabrics. Fat Quarters are approximately 21" x 18" (53 cm x 46 cm).*

CUTTING THE PIECES

Follow **Rotary Cutting**, page 36, to cut fabric. Cut all strips from the selvage-to-selvage width of the fabric. Cutting lengths for borders are exact. All measurements include 1/4" seam allowances.

From assorted light print fabrics:

- Cut 16 **large squares** 5³/₄" x 5³/₄".

From assorted medium print fabrics:

- Cut 1 **small square** 4" x 4".
- Cut 28 **rectangles** 2" x 4".

From blue stripe fabric:

- Cut 2 **top/bottom inner borders** 2" x 25".
- Cut 2 **side inner borders** 2" x 28".

From pink print fabric:

- Cut 2 **top/bottom middle borders** 2" x 28".
- Cut 2 **side middle borders** 2" x 31".

From green print fabric:

- Cut 2 **top/bottom outer borders** 3" x 31".
- Cut 2 **side outer borders** 3" x 36".

From fabric for binding:

- Cut 5 **binding strips** 2¹/₂" wide.

CUTTING THE APPLIQUÉS

Follow **Preparing Fusible Appliqué Pieces**, page 37, and use patterns, pages 10-11, to cut appliqués.

From assorted medium print fabrics:

- Cut 4 **flowers**.
- Cut 4 **flower centers**.

MAKING THE BLOCKS AND SASHINGS

Follow **Piecing** and **Pressing**, page 37, to make Blocks. Use 1/4" seam allowances throughout. Follow **Machine Blanket Stitch Appliqué**, page 38, to add appliqués.

1. Sew 4 **large squares** together to make **Unit 1**. Make 4 Unit 1's.

Unit 1 (make 4)

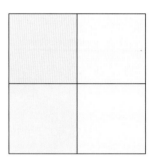

2. Center, fuse, and Blanket Stitch appliqué 1 **flower** and 1 **flower center** to 1 Unit 1 to make **Block**. Make 4 Blocks.

Block (make 4)

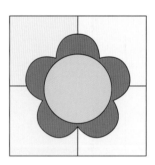

3. Sew 7 **rectangles** together to make **sashing**. Make 4 sashings.

Sashing (make 4)

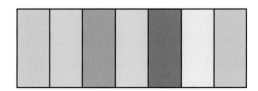

ASSEMBLING THE QUILT TOP CENTER

Refer to Quilt Top Diagram for placement.

1. Sew 2 **Blocks** and 1 **sashing** together to make **Row**. Make 2 Rows.

2. Sew 2 sashings and 1 **small square** together to make **Sashing Row**.

3. Sew Rows and Sashing Row together to make **Quilt Top Center**.

4. Cut rickrack into four 25" lengths. Aligning center of rickrack with the $1/4$" seam allowance of Quilt Top Center, machine baste 1 length of rickrack to each side of Quilt Top Center.

Quilt Top Diagram

ADDING THE BORDERS

1. Matching centers and corners, sew **top/bottom inner borders** to Quilt Top Center.

2. Matching centers and corners, sew **side inner borders** to Quilt Top Center.

3. Remove any exposed basting stitches on rickrack.

4. Repeat Steps 1-2 and to add **middle** and **outer borders** to complete quilt top.

COMPLETING THE QUILT

1. Follow **Quilting**, page 40, to mark, layer, and quilt as desired. Our quilt is machine quilted with meandering in the entire quilt except for the appliquéd flowers. A swirl is quilted in each flower center. *Note: Fold rickrack out of the way while quilting.*

2. Follow **Making a Hanging Sleeve**, page 42, if a hanging sleeve is desired.

3. Follow **Making Straight Grain Binding**, page 44, and use **binding strips** to make binding. Follow **Attaching Binding with Mitered Corners**, page 44, to bind quilt.

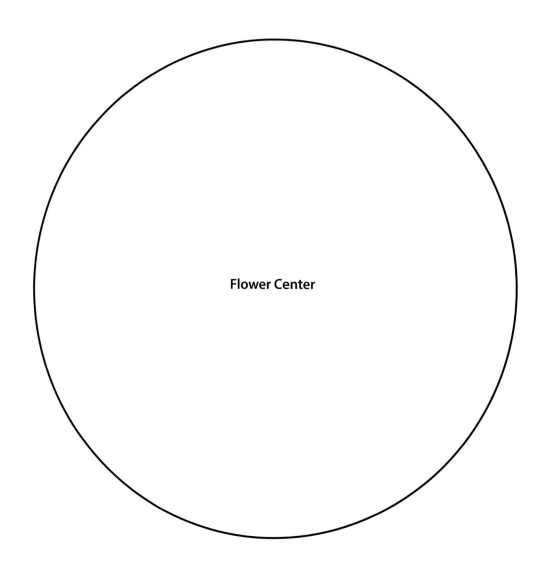

Flower Center

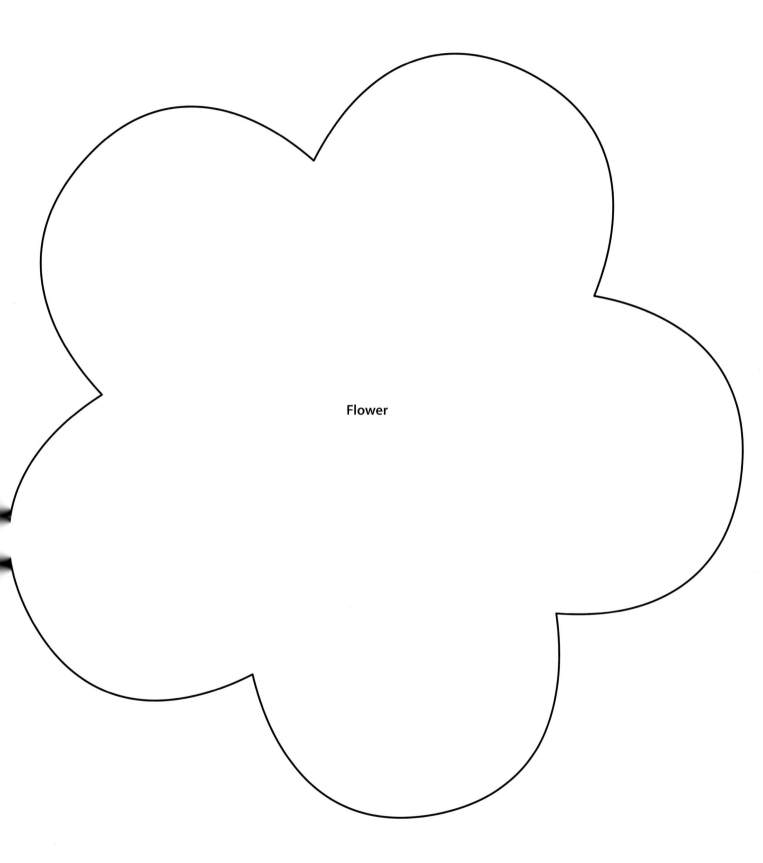

Flower

BABY BOY DOT-TO-DOT

Finished Size: 43" x 43" (109 cm x 109 cm)

Finished Block Size: 6" x 6" (15 cm x 15 cm)

SHOPPING LIST

Yardage is based on 43"/44" (109 cm/112 cm) wide fabric with a usable width of 40" (102 cm).

☐ 1 yd (91 cm) of blue print fabric for blocks

☐ ¹/₄ yd (23 cm) of blue stripe fabric for inner border

☐ 1³/₈ yds (1.3 m) of blue polka dot fabric for blocks and outer border

☐ ¹/₄ yd (23 cm) of blue plaid fabric for blocks

☐ ³/₄ yd (69 cm) of fabric for binding

☐ 2⁷/₈ yds (2.6 m) of fabric for backing

You will also need:

☐ 51" x 51" (130 cm x 130 cm) piece of batting

☐ Paper-backed fusible web

☐ Stabilizer

CUTTING THE PIECES

*Follow **Rotary Cutting**, page 36, to cut fabric. Cut all strips from the selvage-to-selvage width of the fabric unless noted otherwise. Cutting lengths for borders are exact. All measurements include $^1/_4$" seam allowances.*

From blue print fabric:

- Cut 5 strips $6^1/_2$" wide. From these strips, cut 25 **squares** $6^1/_2$" x $6^1/_2$".

From blue stripe fabric:

- Cut 2 **top/bottom inner borders** 2" x $33^1/_2$".
- Cut 2 **side inner borders** 2" x $30^1/_2$".

From blue polka dot fabric:

- Cut 2 *lengthwise* **top/bottom outer borders** 5" x $42^1/_2$".
- Cut 2 *lengthwise* **side outer borders** 5" x $33^1/_2$".

CUTTING THE APPLIQUÉS

*Use the quarter-circle pattern on page 15. The straight edges include seam allowances. Follow **Preparing Fusible Appliqué Pieces**, page 37, to cut appliqués.*

From blue polka dot fabric:

- Cut 25 **quarter-circles**.

From blue plaid fabric:

- Cut 25 **quarter-circles**.

MAKING THE BLOCKS

*Follow **Machine Blanket Stitch Appliqué**, page 38, to make Blocks.*

1. Fuse 1 blue polka dot **quarter-circle** to 1 corner of 1 **square**. Fuse 1 blue plaid quarter-circle to opposite corner of square. Blanket Stitch appliqué quarter-circles to square along curved edges to make Block. Make 25 Blocks.

Block (make 25)

ASSEMBLING THE QUILT TOP CENTER

*Follow **Piecing** and **Pressing**, page 37, to assemble Quilt Top Center. Use $^1/_4$" seam allowances throughout.*

1. Sew 5 **Blocks** together to make Row. Make 5 Rows.

Row (make 5)

2. Referring to Quilt Top Diagram, sew **Rows** together to make **Quilt Top Center**.

ADDING THE BORDERS

1. Matching centers and corners, sew **side inner borders** to Quilt Top Center.
2. Matching centers and corners, sew **top/bottom inner borders** to Quilt Top Center.
3. Repeat Steps 1-2 and to add **side** and then **top/bottom outer borders** to complete quilt top.

COMPLETING THE QUILT

1. Follow **Quilting**, page 40, to mark, layer, and quilt as desired. Our quilt is machine quilted with an all-over loop pattern covering the entire quilt.

2. Follow **Making a Hanging Sleeve**, page 42, if a hanging sleeve is desired.

3. Cut a 23" square of binding fabric. Follow **Making Continuous Bias Binding**, page 43, to make $2^1/_2$" wide bias binding. Follow **Attaching Binding with Mitered Corners**, page 44, to bind quilt.

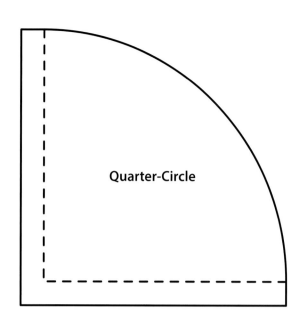

Quarter-Circle

Quilt Top Diagram

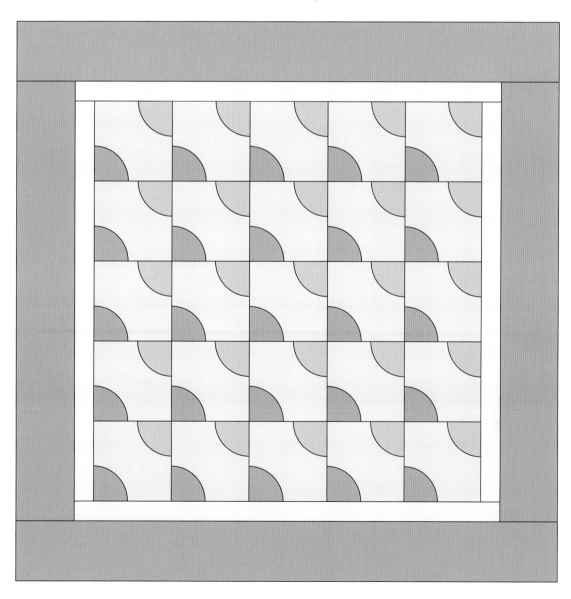

BaBY GIrL DOT-TO-DOT

Finished Size: 43" x 43" (109 cm x 109 cm)

Finished Block Size: 6" x 6" (15 cm x 15 cm)

SHOPPING LIST

Yardage is based on 43"/44" (109 cm/112 cm) wide fabric with a usable width of 40" (102 cm).

- ☐ 1 yd (91 cm) of light print fabric for blocks
- ☐ ¼ yd (23 cm) of pink polka dot fabric for inner border
- ☐ 1⅜ yds (1.3 m) of blue floral fabric for outer border
- ☐ ⅞ yd (80 cm) **total** of assorted print fabrics for blocks
- ☐ ½ yd (46 cm) of fabric for binding
- ☐ 2⅞ yds (2.6 m) of fabric for backing

You will also need:

- ☐ 51" x 51" (130 cm x 130 cm) piece of batting
- ☐ Paper-backed fusible web
- ☐ Stabilizer

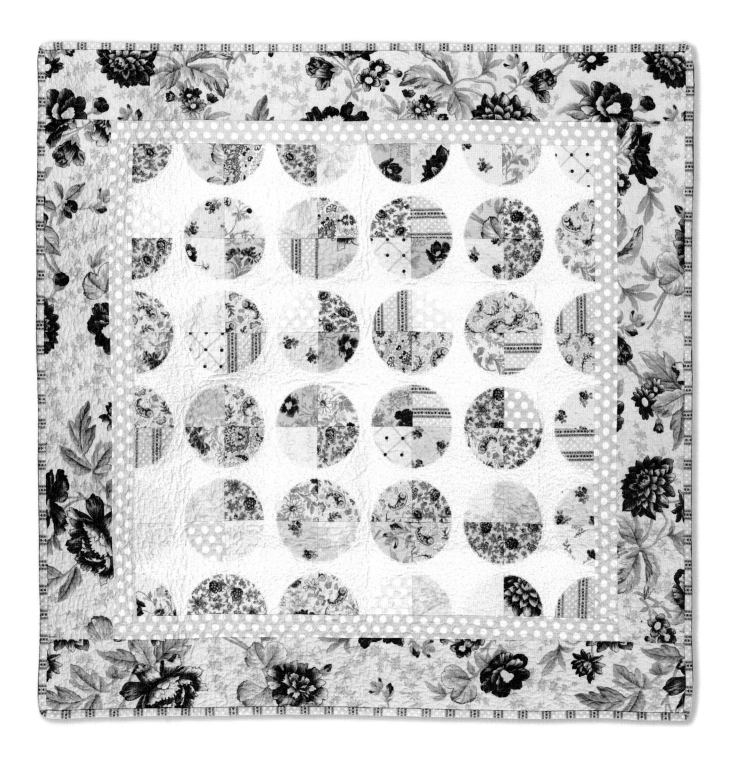

CUTTING THE PIECES

*Follow **Rotary Cutting**, page 36, to cut fabric. Cut all strips from the selvage-to-selvage width of the fabric unless noted otherwise. Cutting lengths for borders are exact. All measurements include $^1/_4$" seam allowances.*

From light print fabric:

- Cut 5 strips $6^1/_2$" wide. From these strips, cut 25 **squares** $6^1/_2$" x $6^1/_2$".

From pink polka dot fabric:

- Cut 2 **top/bottom inner borders** 2" x $33^1/_2$".
- Cut 2 **side inner borders** 2" x $30^1/_2$".

From blue floral fabric:

- Cut 2 *lengthwise* **top/bottom outer borders** 5" x $42^1/_2$".
- Cut 2 *lengthwise* **side outer borders** 5" x $33^1/_2$".

From fabric for binding:

- Cut 5 **binding strips** $2^1/_2$" wide.

CUTTING THE APPLIQUÉS

*Use the quarter-circle pattern on page 19. The straight edges include seam allowances. Follow **Preparing Fusible Appliqué Pieces**, page 37, to cut appliqués.*

From assorted print fabrics:

- Cut 100 **quarter-circles**.

MAKING THE BLOCKS

*Follow **Machine Blanket Stitch Appliqué**, page 38, to make blocks.*

1. Fuse 1 assorted print **quarter-circle** to each corner of 1 **square**. Blanket Stitch appliqué quarter-circles to square along curved edges to make **Block**. Make 25 Blocks.

Block (make 25)

ASSEMBLING THE QUILT TOP CENTER

*Follow **Piecing** and **Pressing**, page 37, to assemble Quilt Top Center. Use $^1/_4$" seam allowances throughout.*

1. Sew 5 **Blocks** together to make **Row**. Make 5 Rows.

Row (make 5)

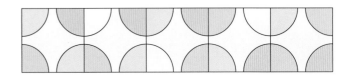

2. Referring to **Quilt Top Diagram**, sew **Rows** together to make **Quilt Top Center**.

ADDING THE BORDERS

1. Matching centers and corners, sew **side inner borders** to Quilt Top Center.
2. Matching centers and corners, sew **top/bottom inner borders** to Quilt Top Center.
3. Repeat Steps 1-2 and to add **side** and then **top/bottom outer borders** to complete quilt top.

COMPLETING THE QUILT

1. Follow **Quilting**, page 40, to mark, layer, and quilt as desired. Our entire quilt is machine meandering quilted.

2. Follow **Making a Hanging Sleeve**, page 42, if a hanging sleeve is desired.

3. Follow **Making Straight Grain Binding**, page 44, and use **binding strips** to make binding. Follow **Attaching Binding with Mitered Corners**, page 44, to bind quilt.

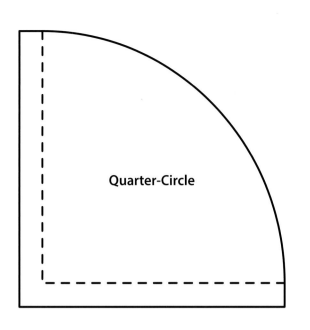

Quarter-Circle

Quilt Top Diagram

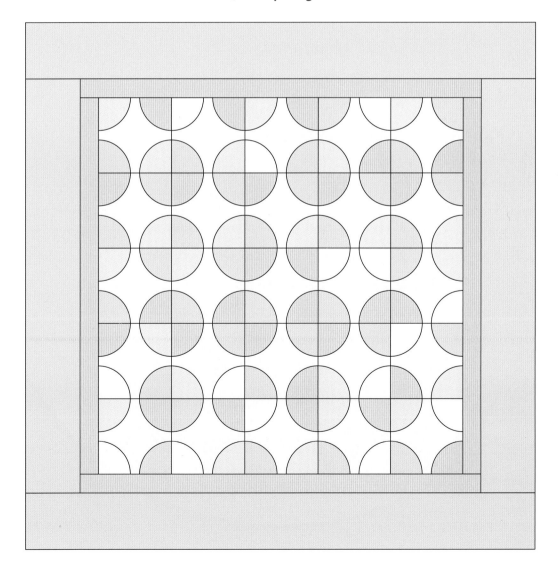

RICKRACK FUN

Finished Size: 39¹/₂" x 44" (100 cm x 112 cm)

*In this quilt-as-you-go design, the strips and rickrack are
stitched onto the quilt layers, so no additional quilting is needed!*

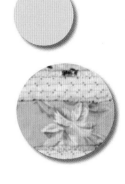

SHOPPING LIST

*Yardage is based on 43"/44" (109 cm/112 cm) wide fabric
with a usable width of 40" (102 cm).*

☐ Jelly Roll* with at least 15 **strips** (includes binding)

☐ 1³/₈ yds (1.3 m) of cream print fabric for quilt top

☐ 2³/₄ yds (2.5 m)† of fabric for backing

You will also need:

☐ 43" x 47¹/₂" (109 cm x 121 cm) rectangle of batting

☐ 4¹/₂ yds (4.1 m) of ⁹/₁₆" (14 mm) wide green rickrack

☐ 2¹/₄ yds (2.1 m) of 1" (25 mm) wide pink rickrack

☐ Quilt basting spray (optional)

☐ Water-soluble fabric marking pen (optional)

***OR** 1¹/₄ yds (1.1 m) *total* of assorted print fabrics. Jelly
Rolls are assortments of 2¹/₂" wide strips.

† If usable width of fabric is 43" or larger, 1³/₈ yds
(1.3 m) will be adequate.

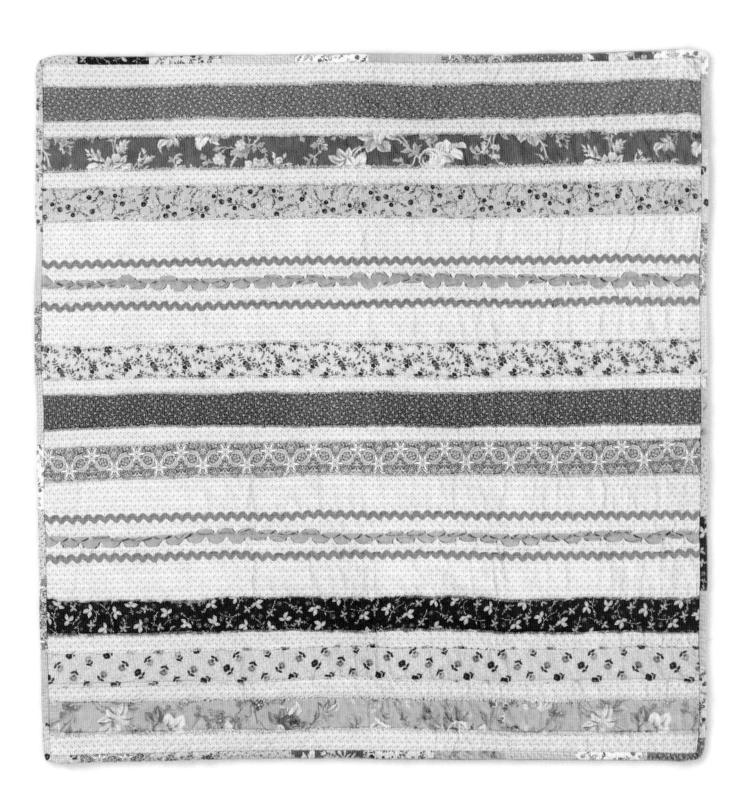

CUTTING THE PIECES

*Follow **Rotary Cutting**, page 36, to cut fabric. Cut all strips from the selvage-to-selvage width of the fabric. All measurements include $^1/_4$" seam allowances.*

From cream print fabric:

- Cut 1 **quilt top** 39" x 43$^1/_2$".

From fabric for backing:

- Cut 1 **backing** 43" x 47$^1/_2$", pieced as needed.

From assorted fabrics:

- Cut 15 **strips** 2$^1/_2$" wide if not using Jelly Roll.

LAYERING THE QUILT SANDWICH

1. Lay backing, right side down, on a flat surface.
2. If using basting spray, follow manufacturer's instructions to baste batting to backing. Baste quilt top, right side up and centered, to batting to make quilt sandwich. (If not using basting spray, use safety pins to "pin-baste" layers together.)

ADDING THE STRIPS AND RICKRACK

Refer to Quilt Diagram for placement.

1. Cut rickrack into 39" lengths: 4 green and 2 pink.
2. Trim 9 **strips** to 39" long. Arrange strips and rickrack as shown and pin in place. ***Tip:*** *It may be helpful to mark placement lines on quilt top with water-soluble fabric pen.* Topstitch strips $^1/_4$" from long raw edges, stitching through all layers. Topstitch in center of rickrack, stitching through all layers.

COMPLETING THE QUILT

1. From remaining 6 strips, cut a *total* of 42 **binding strips** 2$^1/_2$" x 5". Matching short edges, sew binding strips together to make binding. Press binding in half lengthwise.
2. Follow **Making a Hanging Sleeve**, page 42, if a hanging sleeve is desired.
3. Follow **Attaching Binding with Mitered Corners**, page 44, to bind quilt.
4. Machine wash and dry quilt to fray raw edges.

Quilt Diagram

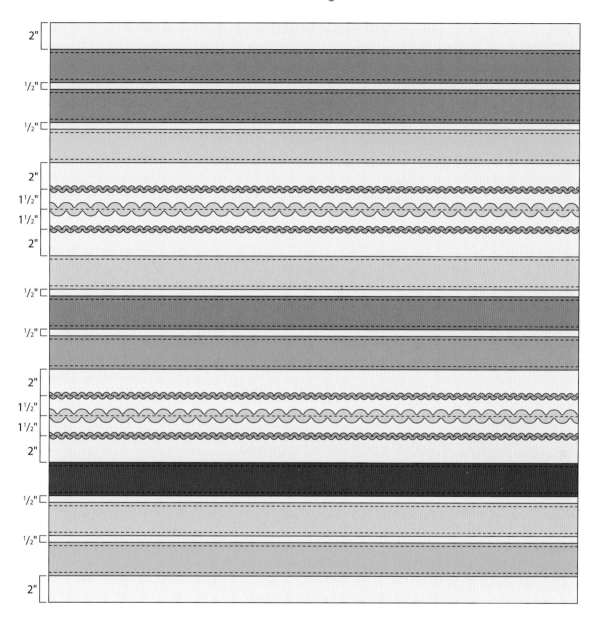

2"

½"

½"

2"
1½"
1½"
2"

½"

½"

2"
1½"
1½"
2"

½"

½"

2"

FLOWERS

Finished Size: 41" x 41" (104 cm x 104 cm)

In this quilt-as-you-go design, the strips and flowers are stitched onto the quilt layers, so no additional quilting is needed!

SHOPPING LIST

Yardage is based on 43"/44" (109 cm/112 cm) wide fabric with a usable width of 40" (102 cm).

☐ Jelly Roll* with at least 17 **strips**

☐ Charm Packs* with at least 50 **squares**

☐ 2³/₈ yds (2.2 m)† of cream print fabric for quilt top

☐ 2¹/₂ yds (2.3 m) of fabric for backing

You will also need:

☐ 45" x 45" (114 cm x 114 cm) piece of batting

☐ Template plastic

☐ Quilt basting spray (optional)

☐ Water-soluble fabric pen (optional)

***OR** 2 yds (1.8 m) **total** of assorted print fabrics. Jelly Rolls are assortments of 2¹/₂" wide strips. Charm Packs are assortments of 5" x 5" squares.

† If usable width of fabric is 41" or larger, 1¹/₄ yds (1.1 m) will be adequate.

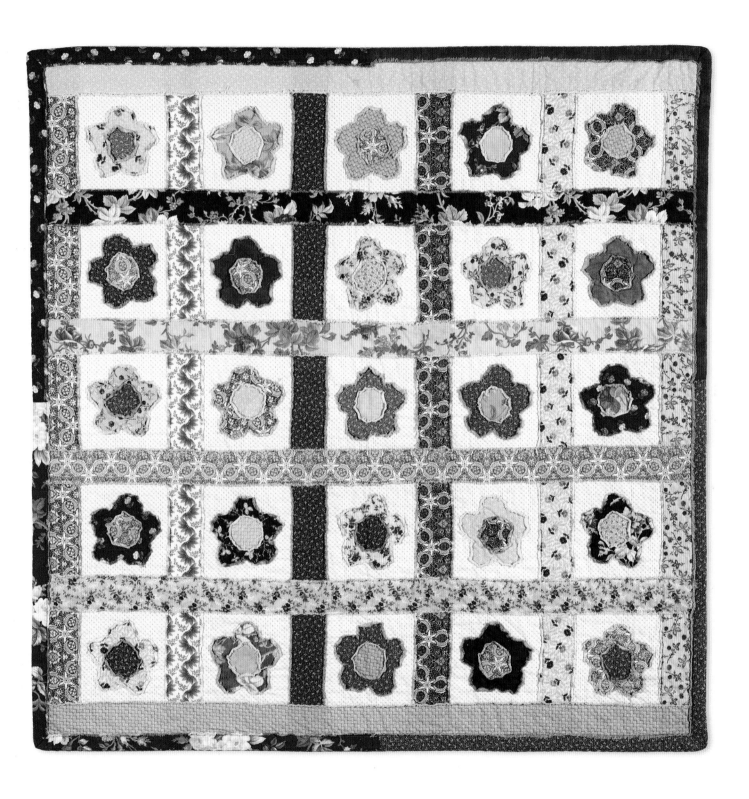

CUTTING THE PIECES

*Follow **Rotary Cutting**, page 36, to cut fabric. Cut all strips from the selvage-to-selvage width of the fabric. All measurements include ¹/₄" seam allowances.*

From cream print fabric:
- Cut quilt top 41" x 41", pieced as needed.

From fabric for backing:
- Cut backing 45" x 45", pieced as needed.

From assorted fabrics:
- Cut 17 **strips** 2¹/₂" wide if not using Jelly Roll.

CUTTING THE APPLIQUÉS

*Follow **Template Cutting**, page 36, and use patterns, page 29, to cut appliqués.*

From Charm Packs or assorted print fabrics:
- Cut 25 **flowers**.
- Cut 25 **flower centers**.

LAYERING THE QUILT SANDWICH

1. Lay backing, right side down, on a flat surface.
2. If using basting spray, follow manufacturer's instructions to baste batting to backing. Baste quilt top, right side up and centered, to batting to make quilt sandwich. (If not using basting spray, use safety pins to "pin-baste" layers together.)

ADDING THE STRIPS AND FLOWERS

*Refer to **Quilt Diagram**, page 28, for placement.*

1. Trim 12 **strips** to 41" long. Arrange 6 strips vertically as shown and pin in place. ***Tip:*** *It may be helpful to mark placement lines on quilt top with water-soluble fabric pen.* Topstitch strips ¹/₄" from long raw edges, stitching through all layers.
2. Arrange 6 strips horizontally as shown and pin in place. Topstitch strips ¹/₄" from long raw edges, stitching through all layers.
3. Making sure **flowers** are placed the same, center and pin 1 flower to each area between strips. Topstitch flowers ¹/₄" from raw edges, stitching through all layers.
4. Center and pin 1 **flower center** to each flower. Topstitch flower centers ¹/₄" from raw edges, stitching through all layers.

COMPLETING THE QUILT

1. Trim backing and batting even with quilt top.
2. Sew 5 strips, end to end, to make binding. Press binding in half lengthwise.
3. Leaving approximately 10" of binding loose and beginning near center of one edge of quilt, place binding over edge of quilt to enclose raw edges of quilt and pin, stopping at corner of quilt (**Fig. 1**).

Fig. 1

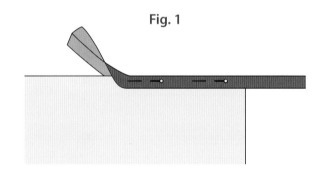

4. At the corner, fold binding as shown in **Fig. 2** to form miter. Finger press miter on corner and pin.

Fig. 2

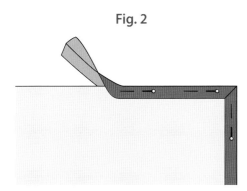

5. Continue pinning binding around quilt, mitering corners and stopping approximately 8" from beginning.
6. Leaving the ends of binding unstitched, topstitch through all layers, sewing binding to front and back of quilt $1/4$" from raw edges of binding. Lift needle out of fabric and clip thread.
7. Bring the ends of binding to center of opening and fold each end back (**Fig. 3**). Finger press folds.

Fig. 3

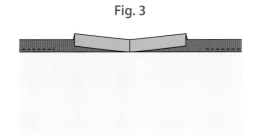

8. Unfold ends of binding and draw a line on wrong side in each finger-pressed crease.
9. Matching right sides and drawn lines, pin binding ends together (**Fig. 4**).

Fig. 4

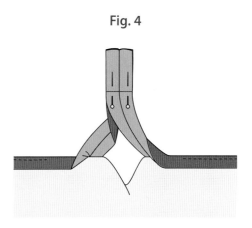

10. Stitch along drawn lines, removing pins as you stitch.
11. Lay binding against quilt to ensure correct length. Trim seam allowances and finish topstitching binding to quilt.
12. Machine wash and dry quilt to fray raw edges.

Quilt Diagram

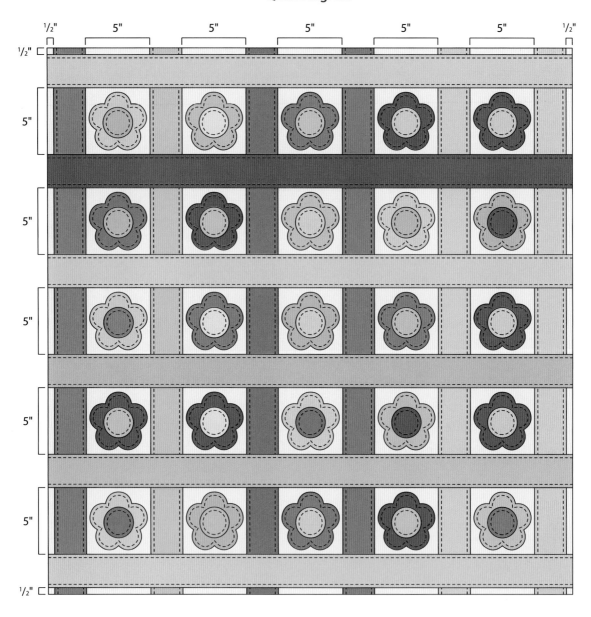

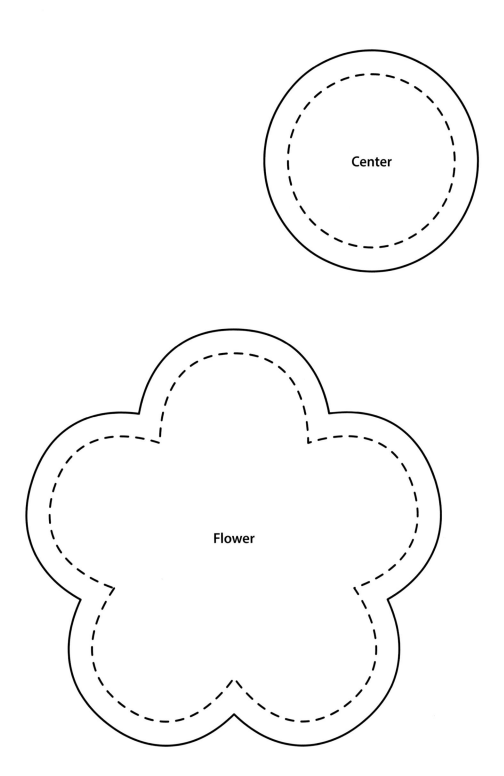

Center

Flower

stars

Finished Size: 40½" x 40½" (103 cm x 103 cm) including Prairie Points

Finished Block Size: 6" x 6" (15 cm x 15 cm)

SHOPPING LIST

Yardage is based on 43"/44" (109 cm/112 cm) wide fabric with a usable width of 40" (102 cm).

☐ ¾ yd (69 cm) of red dot fabric

☐ ¾ yd (69 cm) of red check fabric

☐ 1 yd (91 cm) of white/red print fabric

☐ ½ yd (46 cm) of red print fabric for border

☐ 18" x 24" (46 cm x 61 cm) rectangle of red solid felted wool fabric

☐ 16" x 20" (41 cm x 51 cm) rectangle of white solid felted wool fabric

☐ 40" x 40" (102 cm x 102 cm) square of fabric for backing

You will also need:

☐ 40" x 40" (102 cm x 102 cm) square of batting

☐ Red and white embroidery floss

☐ Freezer paper

CUTTING THE PIECES

*Follow **Rotary Cutting**, page 36, to cut fabric. Cut all strips from the selvage-to-selvage width of the fabric. Cutting lengths for borders are exact. All measurements include $1/4$" seam allowances.*

From red dot fabric:

- Cut 2 strips 5" wide. From these strips, cut 10 **medium squares** 5" x 5".
- Cut 3 strips $3^1/_2$" wide. From these strips, cut 24 **small squares** $3^1/_2$" x $3^1/_2$".

From red check fabric:

- Cut 2 strips 5" wide. From these strips, cut 11 **medium squares** 5" x 5".
- Cut 3 strips $3^1/_2$" wide. From these strips, cut 24 **small squares** $3^1/_2$" x $3^1/_2$".

From white/red print fabric:

- Cut 3 strips $6^1/_2$" wide. From these strips, cut 13 **large squares** $6^1/_2$" x $6^1/_2$".
- Cut 2 strips 5" wide. From these strips, cut 11 **medium squares** 5" x 5".

From red print fabric:

- Cut 2 **top/bottom borders** $3^1/_2$" x $30^1/_2$".
- Cut 2 **side borders** $3^1/_2$" x $36^1/_2$".

CUTTING THE APPLIQUÉS

Trace patterns, page 34, onto dull side of freezer paper and cut out on traced lines to make templates. Iron templates, shiny side down, to right side of wool and cut out appliqués. Use templates as many times as possible before cutting additional templates.

From red solid wool fabric:

- Cut 13 **circles**.

From white solid wool fabric:

- Cut 13 **stars**.

MAKING THE STAR BLOCKS

1. Center 1 **circle** on 1 **large square** and pin in place. Appliqué circle to large square using 3 strands of red embroidery floss and Blanket Stitch, page 46.
2. Referring to **Star Block** diagram for placement, pin 1 **star** on 1 circle. Appliqué star to circle using 2 strands of white embroidery floss and Blanket Stitch.
3. Repeat Steps 1-2 to make 13 **Star Blocks**.

Star Block (make 13)

MAKING THE 4-PATCH BLOCKS

*Follow **Piecing** and **Pressing**, page 37, to make 4-Patch Blocks. Use $1/4$" seam allowances throughout.*

1. Sew 1 red dot **small square** and 1 red check small square together to make **Unit 1**. Make 24 Unit 1's.

Unit 1 (make 24)

2. Sew 2 **Unit 1's** together to make 4-Patch Block. Make 12 4-Patch Blocks.

4-Patch Block (make 12)

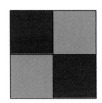

ASSEMBLING THE QUILT TOP

Refer to Quilt Diagram for placement.

1. Sew 3 **Star Blocks** and 2 **4-Patch Blocks** together to make **Row A**. Make 3 Row A's.

2. Sew 2 Star Blocks and 3 4-Patch Blocks together to make **Row B**. Make 2 Row B's.

3. Alternating Row A's and Row B's, sew Rows together to make **Quilt Top Center**.

4. Matching centers and corners, sew **top/bottom borders** to Quilt Top Center.

5. Matching centers and corners, sew **side borders** to Quilt Top Center to complete quilt top.

Quilt Diagram

33

COMPLETING THE QUILT

1. Follow **Quilting**, page 40, to mark, layer, and quilt the quilt center *only. (Do not quilt the border at this time.)* Our quilt is machine quilted. The stars are outline quilted and the circles are echo quilted. The rest of the quilt center is quilted with a continuous loop and star pattern. The outer edge of the quilt center is quilted in the ditch.

2. Trim batting and backing same size as quilt top.

3. For each **Prairie Point**, fold 1 **medium square** in half diagonally and then fold in half again; press. Make 32 Prairie Points.

4. Prairie Points will be sewn to quilt top and batting. Fold and pin backing out of the way on all sides.

5. Matching right sides and raw edges, evenly space 8 **Prairie Points** on each edge of quilt top, overlapping as needed; pin. Sew Prairie Points to quilt top and batting. Press Prairie Points to outside.

6. Smooth out backing behind borders. Covering stitching line, fold backing edges 1/4" to wrong side and pin. Blind Stitch backing to Prairie Points.

7. Quilt the border as desired. Our borders are quilted with a continuous loop and star pattern.

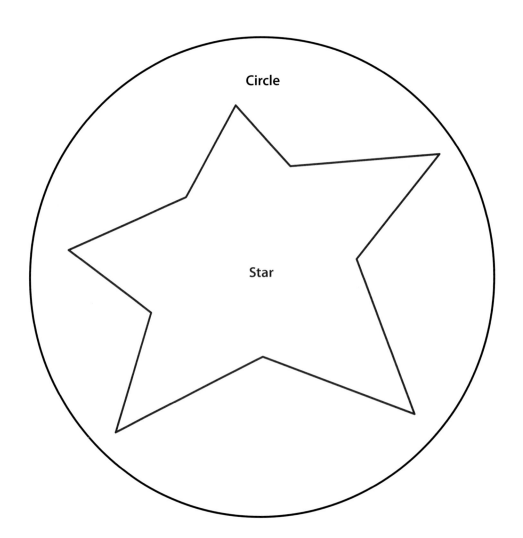

General Instructions

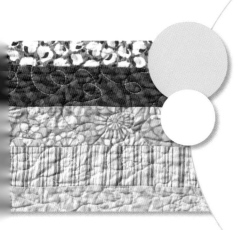
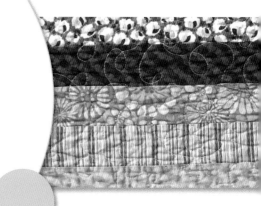

To make your quilting easier and more enjoyable, we encourage you to carefully read all of the general instructions, study the color photographs, and familiarize yourself with the individual project instructions before beginning a project.

FABRICS

SELECTING FABRICS

Choose high-quality, medium-weight 100% cotton fabrics. All-cotton fabrics hold a crease better, fray less, and are easier to quilt than cotton/polyester blends.

Yardage requirements listed for each project are based on 43"/44" wide fabric with a "usable" width of 40" after shrinkage and trimming selvages. Actual usable width will probably vary slightly from fabric to fabric. Our recommended yardage lengths should be adequate for occasional re-squaring of fabric when many cuts are required.

PREPARING FABRICS

For projects using pre-cut fabric pieces, such as Jelly Rolls and Charm Packs, we do not recommend pre-washing fabrics. For other projects, you may wish to pre-wash fabrics to prevent shrinkage and fading.

ROTARY CUTTING

Rotary cutting has brought speed and accuracy to quiltmaking by allowing quilters to easily cut strips of fabric and then cut those strips into smaller pieces.

• Place fabric on work surface with fold closest to you.

• Cut all strips from the selvage-to-selvage width of the fabric unless otherwise indicated in project instructions.

• Square left edge of fabric using rotary cutter and rulers (Figs. 1-2).

Fig. 1

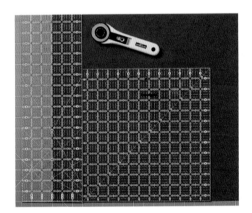

Fig. 2

• To cut each strip required for a project, place ruler over cut edge of fabric, aligning desired marking on ruler with cut edge; make cut (Fig. 3).

Fig. 3

• When cutting several strips from a single piece of fabric, it is important to make sure that cuts remain at a perfect right angle to the fold; square fabric as needed.

TEMPLATE CUTTING

Our patterns for templates have two lines: a solid outer line for cutting and a dashed line 1/4" from outer line for stitching.

1. To make a template from a pattern, use a permanent fine-point pen to carefully trace pattern onto template plastic. Cut out template along inner edge of drawn line. Check template against original pattern for accuracy.

2. Place template face down on wrong side of fabric. Use a sharp fabric marking pencil to draw around template. Use scissors to cut out fabric pieces along drawn line.

PIECING

Precise cutting, followed by accurate piecing, will ensure that all pieces of quilt top fit together well.

- Set sewing machine stitch length for approximately 11 stitches per inch.

- Use neutral-colored general-purpose sewing thread (not quilting thread) in needle and in bobbin.

- An accurate $1/4$" seam allowance is **essential**. Presser feet that are $1/4$" wide are available for most sewing machines.

- When piecing, place pieces right sides together and match raw edges; pin if necessary.

- Chain piecing saves time and will usually result in more accurate piecing.

- Trim away points of seam allowances that extend beyond edges of sewn pieces.

SEWING ACROSS SEAM INTERSECTIONS

When sewing across intersection of two seams, place pieces right sides together and match seams exactly, making sure seam allowances are pressed in opposite directions (Fig. 4).

Fig. 4

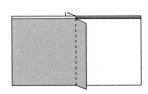

PRESSING

- Use steam iron set on "Cotton" for all pressing.

- Press after sewing each seam.

- Seam allowances are almost always pressed to one side, usually toward darker fabric. However, to reduce bulk it may occasionally be necessary to press seam allowances toward the lighter fabric or even to press them open.

- To prevent dark fabric seam allowance from showing through light fabric, trim darker seam allowance slightly narrower than lighter seam allowance.

- To press long seams without curving or other distortion, lay seams across width of the ironing board.

APPLIQUÉ

PREPARING FUSIBLE APPLIQUÉ PIECES

White or light-colored fabrics may need to be lined with fusible interfacing before applying fusible web to prevent darker fabrics from showing through.

1. Place paper-backed fusible web, paper side up, over appliqué pattern. Trace pattern onto paper side of web with pencil as many times as indicated in project instructions for a single fabric.

2. Follow manufacturer's instructions to fuse traced patterns to wrong side of fabrics. Do not remove paper backing.

3. Use scissors to cut out appliqué pieces along traced lines. Remove paper backing from all pieces.

MACHINE BLANKET STITCH APPLIQUÉ

Some sewing machines feature a Blanket Stitch similar to the one used in this book. Refer to your owner's manual for machine set-up. If your machine does not have this stitch, try a medium-width zigzag or any of the decorative stitches your machine has until you are satisfied with the look.

1. Thread sewing machine with general-purpose thread; use general-purpose thread that matches background fabric in bobbin.

2. Attach an open-toe presser foot. Select far right needle position and needle down (if your machine has this feature).

3. Pin stabilizer, such as paper or any of the commercially available products, to wrong side of background fabric.

4. Bring bobbin thread to the top of the fabric by lowering then raising the needle, bringing up the bobbin thread loop. Pull the loop all the way to the surface.

5. Begin by stitching 5 or 6 stitches in place (drop feed dogs or set stitch length at 0) or, if available, use your machine's lock stitch feature, to anchor thread. Return setting to selected Blanket Stitch.

6. Most of the Blanket Stitch should be done on the appliqué with the right edges of the stitch falling at the very outside edge of the appliqué. Stitch over all exposed raw edges of appliqué pieces.

7. (*Note:* Dots on **Figs. 5-9** indicate where to leave needle in fabric when pivoting.) Always stopping with the needle down in background fabric, refer to **Fig. 5** to stitch outside points, such as the tips of leaves. Stop 1 stitch short of point. Raise presser foot. Pivot project slightly, lower presser foot, and make angled **Stitch 1**. Take next stitch, stop at point, and pivot so **Stitch 2** will be straight into the point. Pivot slightly to make **Stitch 3**. Continue stitching.

Fig. 5

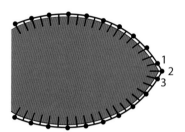

8. For outside corners (**Fig. 6**), stitch to corner, stopping with needle in background fabric. Raise presser foot. Pivot project, lower presser foot, and take an angled stitch. Raise presser foot. Pivot project, lower presser foot and stitch adjacent side.

Fig. 6

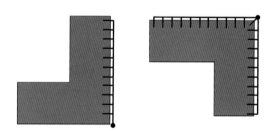

9. For inside corners (Fig. 7), stitch to the corner, taking the last bite at the corner and stopping with the needle down in background fabric. Raise presser foot. Pivot project, lower presser foot, and take an angled stitch. Raise presser foot. Pivot project, lower presser foot and stitch adjacent side.

Fig. 7

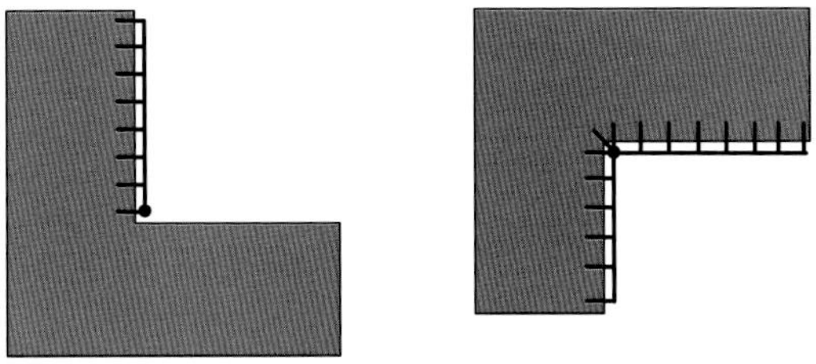

10. When stitching outside curves (Fig. 8), stop with needle in background fabric. Raise presser foot and pivot project as needed. Lower presser foot and continue stitching, pivoting as often as necessary to follow curve.

Fig. 8

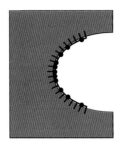

11. When stitching inside curves (Fig. 9), stop with needle in background fabric. Raise presser foot and pivot project as needed. Lower presser foot and continue stitching, pivoting as often as necessary to follow curve.

Fig. 9

12. When stopping stitching, use a needle to pull threads to wrong side of background fabric (Fig. 10); knot, then trim ends, or use a lock stitch to sew 5 or 6 stitches in place.

Fig. 10

13. Carefully tear away stabilizer.

QUILTING

*Quilting holds the three layers (top, batting, and backing) of the quilt together and can be done by hand or machine. Because marking, layering, and quilting are interrelated and may be done in different orders depending on circumstances, please read entire **Quilting** section, pages 40-42, before beginning project.*

TYPES OF QUILTING DESIGNS

In the Ditch Quilting

Quilting along seamlines or along edges of appliquéd pieces is called "in the ditch" quilting. This type of quilting should be done on side **opposite** seam allowance and does not have to be marked.

Outline Quilting

Quilting a consistent distance, usually ¹/₄", from seam or appliqué is called "outline" quilting. Outline quilting may be marked or ¹/₄" masking tape may be placed along seamlines for quilting guide. (Do not leave tape on quilt longer than necessary, since it may leave an adhesive residue.)

Motif Quilting

Quilting a design, such as a feathered wreath, is called "motif" quilting. This type of quilting should be marked before basting quilt layers together.

Echo Quilting

Quilting that follows the outline of an appliquéd or pieced design with two or more parallel lines is called "echo" quilting. This type of quilting does not need to be marked.

Meandering Quilting

Quilting in random curved lines and swirls is called "meandering" quilting. Quilting lines should not cross or touch each other. This type of quilting does not need to be marked.

Stipple Quilting

Meandering quilting that is very closely spaced is called "stipple" quilting. Stippling will flatten the area quilted and is often stitched in background areas to raise appliquéd or pieced designs. This type of quilting does not need to be marked.

MARKING QUILTING LINES

Quilting lines may be marked using fabric marking pencils, chalk markers, or water- or air-soluble pens.

Simple quilting designs may be marked with chalk or chalk pencil after basting. A small area may be marked, then quilted, before moving to next area to be marked. Intricate designs should be marked before basting using a more durable marker.

Caution: Pressing may permanently set some marks. **Test** different markers **on scrap fabric** to find one that marks clearly and can be thoroughly removed.

A wide variety of pre-cut quilting stencils, as well as entire books of quilting patterns, are available. Using a stencil makes it easier to mark intricate or repetitive designs.

To make a stencil from a pattern, center template plastic over pattern and use a permanent marker to trace pattern onto plastic. Use a craft knife with single or double blade to cut channels along traced lines (Fig. 11).

Fig. 11

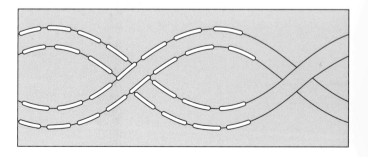

PREPARING THE BACKING

To allow for slight shifting of quilt top during quilting, backing should be larger than the quilt top. Prepare backing the same size as batting called for in project. To piece a backing using 43"/44" wide fabric, use the following instructions.

1. Cut backing fabric into two lengths slightly longer than *length* of batting called for in project. Trim selvages. Place lengths with right sides facing and sew long edges together, forming tube **(Fig. 12)**. Match seams and press along one fold **(Fig. 13)**. Cut along pressed fold to form single piece **(Fig. 14)**.

Fig. 12   Fig. 13

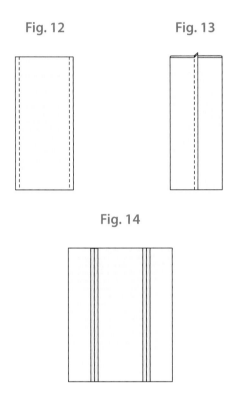

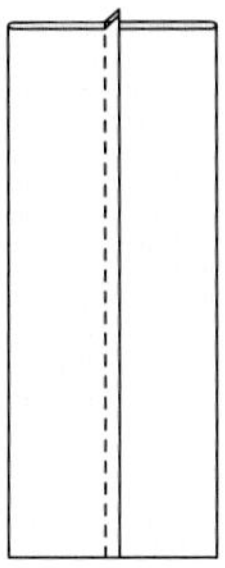

Fig. 14

.   Trim backing to same size as batting; press seam allowances open.

CHOOSING THE BATTING

The appropriate batting will make quilting easier. For fine hand quilting, choose low-loft batting. All cotton or cotton/polyester blend battings work well for machine quilting because the cotton helps "grip" quilt layers. If quilt is to be tied, a high-loft batting, sometimes called extra-loft or fat batting, may be used to make quilt "fluffy."

Types of batting include cotton, polyester, cotton/polyester blend, wool, cotton/wool blend, and silk.

When selecting batting, refer to package labels for characteristics and care instructions. Cut batting the size called for in project.

ASSEMBLING THE QUILT

1. Examine wrong side of quilt top closely; trim any seam allowances and clip any threads that may show through front of the quilt. Press quilt top, being careful not to "set" any marked quilting lines.

2. Place backing *wrong* side up on flat surface. Use masking tape to tape edges of backing to surface. Place batting on top of backing fabric. Smooth batting gently, being careful not to stretch or tear. Center quilt top *right* side up on batting.

3. Use 1" rustproof safety pins to "pin-baste" all layers together, spacing pins approximately 4" apart. Begin at center and work toward outer edges to secure all layers. If possible, place pins away from areas that will be quilted, although pins may be removed as needed when quilting.

MACHINE QUILTING METHODS

Use general-purpose thread in bobbin. Do not use quilting thread. Thread the needle of machine with general-purpose thread or transparent monofilament thread to make quilting blend with quilt top fabrics. Use decorative thread, such as a metallic or contrasting-color general-purpose thread, to make quilting lines stand out more.

Straight-Line Quilting

The term "straight-line" is somewhat deceptive, since curves (especially gentle ones) as well as straight lines can be stitched with this technique.

1. Set stitch length for 6 to 10 stitches per inch and attach walking foot to sewing machine.

2. Determine which section of quilt will have longest continuous quilting line, oftentimes area from center top to center bottom. Roll up and secure each edge of quilt to help reduce the bulk, keeping fabrics smooth. Smaller projects may not need to be rolled.

3. Begin stitching on longest quilting line, using very short stitches for the first $1/4$" to "lock" quilting. Stitch across project, using one hand on each side of walking foot to slightly spread fabric and to guide fabric through machine. Lock stitches at end of quilting line.

4. Continue machine quilting, stitching longer quilting lines first to stabilize quilt before moving on to other areas.

Free-Motion Quilting

Free-motion quilting may be free form or may follow a marked pattern.

1. Attach darning foot to sewing machine and lower or cover feed dogs.

2. Position quilt under darning foot; lower foot. Holding top thread, take a stitch and pull bobbin thread to top of quilt. To "lock" beginning of quilting line, hold top and bobbin threads while making 3 to 5 stitches in place.

3. Use one hand on each side of darning foot to move fabric through the machine. Even stitch length is achieved by using smooth, flowing hand motion and steady machine speed. Slow machine speed and fast hand movement will create long stitches. Fast machine speed and slow hand movement will create short stitches. Move quilt sideways, back and forth, in a circular motion, or in a random motion to create desired designs; do not rotate quilt. Lock stitches at end of each quilting line.

MAKING A HANGING SLEEVE

Attaching a hanging sleeve to back of wall hanging or quilt before the binding is added allows project to be displayed on wall.

1. Measure width of quilt top edge and subtract 1". Cut piece of fabric 7" wide by determined measurement.

2. Press short edges of fabric piece $1/4$" to wrong side; press edges $1/4$" to wrong side again and machine stitch in place.

3. Matching wrong sides, fold piece in half lengthwise to form tube.

4. Follow project instructions to sew binding to quilt top and to trim backing and batting. Before Blindstitching binding to backing, match raw edges and stitch hanging sleeve to center top edge on back of quilt.

5. Finish binding quilt, treating hanging sleeve as part of backing.

6. Blindstitch bottom of hanging sleeve to backing, taking care not to stitch through to front of quilt.

7. Insert dowel or slat into hanging sleeve.

BINDING

MAKING CONTINUOUS BIAS BINDING

Bias strips for binding can simply be cut and pieced to desired length. However, when a long length of binding is needed, the "continuous" method is quick and accurate.

1. Cut square from binding fabric the size indicated in project instructions. Cut square in half diagonally to make two triangles.

2. With right sides together and using $^1/_4$" seam allowance, sew triangles together (Fig. 15); press seam allowances open.

Fig. 15

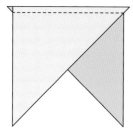

On wrong side of fabric, draw lines the width of binding as specified in project instructions, usually $2^1/_2$" (Fig. 16). Cut off any remaining fabric less than this width.

Fig. 16

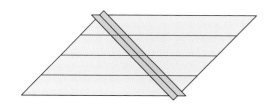

4. With right sides inside, bring short edges together to form tube; match raw edges so that first drawn line of top section meets second drawn line of bottom section (Fig. 17).

Fig. 17

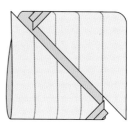

5. Carefully pin edges together by inserting pins through drawn lines at point where drawn lines intersect, making sure pins go through intersections on both sides. Using $^1/_4$" seam allowance, sew edges together; press seam allowances open.

6. To cut continuous strip, begin cutting along first drawn line (Fig. 18). Continue cutting along drawn line around tube.

Fig. 18

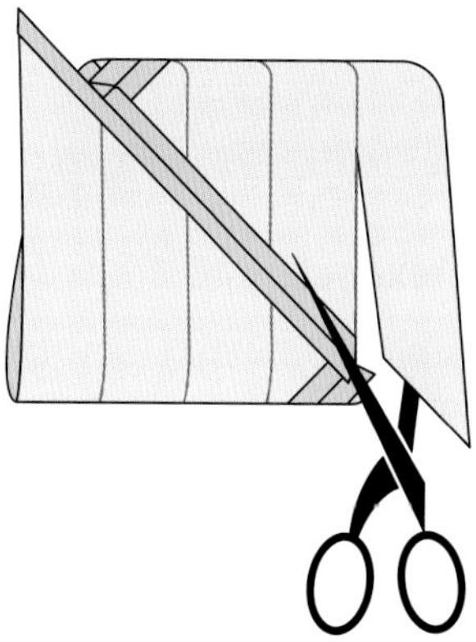

7. Trim ends of bias strip square.

8. Matching wrong sides and raw edges, carefully press bias strip in half lengthwise to complete binding.

MAKING STRAIGHT-GRAIN BINDING

1. Sew binding strips called for in project together, end to end, into 1 continuous length.

2. Matching wrong sides and raw edges, carefully press continuous strip in half lengthwise to complete binding.

ATTACHING BINDING WITH MITERED CORNERS

1. Beginning with one end near center on bottom edge of quilt, lay binding around quilt to make sure that seams in binding will not end up at a corner. Adjust placement if necessary. Matching raw edges of binding to raw edge of quilt top, pin binding to right side of quilt along one edge.

2. When you reach first corner, mark 1/4" from corner of quilt top (Fig. 19).

Fig. 19

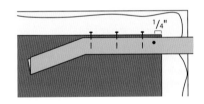

3. Beginning approximately 10" from end of binding and using 1/4" seam allowance, sew binding to quilt, backstitching at beginning of stitching and at mark (Fig. 20). Lift needle out of fabric and clip thread.

Fig. 20

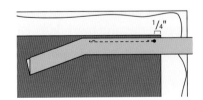

4. Fold binding as shown in Figs. 21-22 and pin binding to adjacent side, matching raw edges. When you've reached the next corner, mark 1/4" from edge of quilt top.

Fig. 21

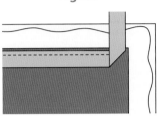

Fig. 22

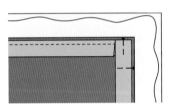

5. Backstitching at edge of quilt top, sew pinned binding to quilt (Fig. 23); backstitch at the next mark. Lift needle out of fabric and clip thread.

Fig. 23

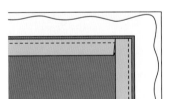

6. Continue sewing binding to quilt, stopping approximately 10" from starting point (Fig. 24).

Fig. 24

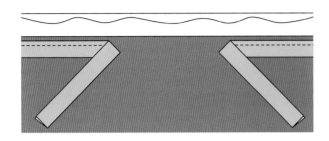

7. Bring beginning and end of binding to center of opening and fold each end back, leaving a 1/4" space between folds (Fig. 25). Finger press folds.

Fig. 25

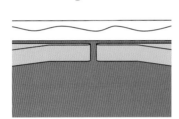

8. Unfold ends of binding and draw a line across wrong side in finger-pressed crease. Draw a line through the lengthwise pressed fold of binding at the same spot to create a cross mark. With edge of ruler at cross mark, line up 45° angle marking on ruler with one long side of binding. Draw a diagonal line from edge to edge. Repeat on remaining end, making sure that the two diagonal lines are angled the same way (Fig. 26).

Fig. 26

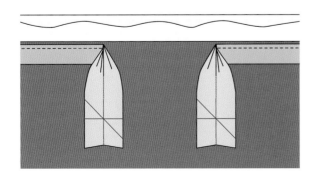

9. Matching right sides and diagonal lines, pin binding ends together a right angles (Fig. 27).

Fig. 27

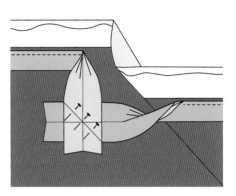

10. Machine stitch along diagonal line (Fig. 28), removing pins as you stitch.

Fig. 28

11. Lay binding against quilt to double check that it is correct length.
12. Trim binding ends, leaving 1/4" seam allowance; press seam open. Stitch binding to quilt.
13. Trim backing and batting a scan 1/4" larger on all sides than quilt top.

14. On one edge of quilt, fold binding over to quilt backing and pin pressed edge in place, covering stitching line (Fig. 29). On adjacent side, fold binding over, forming a mitered corner (Fig. 30). Repeat to pin remainder of binding in place.

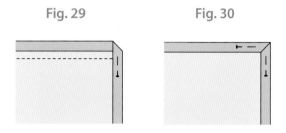

Fig. 29   Fig. 30

15. Blindstitch (next column) binding to backing, taking care not to stitch through to front of quilt.

SIGNING AND DATING YOUR QUILT

A completed quilt is a work of art and should be signed and dated. There are many different ways to do this and numerous books on the subject. The label should reflect the style of the quilt, the occasion or person for which it was made, and the quilter's own particular talents. Following are suggestions for recording the history of your quilt or adding a sentiment for future generations.

- Embroider quilter's name, date, and any additional information on quilt top or backing.

- Make label from muslin and use permanent marker to write information. Use different colored permanent markers to make label more decorative. Stitch label to back of quilt.

- Use photo-transfer paper to add image to white or cream fabric label. Stitch label to back of quilt.

- Make an extra block from quilt top pattern to use as label. Add information with permanent fabric pen. Appliqué block to back of quilt.

- Write message on appliquéd design from quilt top. Attach appliqué to back of the quilt.

HAND STITCHES

BLANKET STITCH

Come up at 1, go down at 2, and come up at 3, keeping thread below point of needle (Fig. 31).

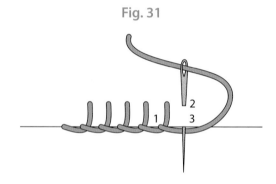

Fig. 31

BLIND STITCH

Come up at 1, go down at 2, and come up at 3 (Fig. 32). Length of stitches may be varied as desired.

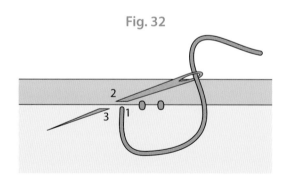

Fig. 32

meet the designer

BONNIE OLAVESON

As Bonnie Olaveson knows, the love of creativity just naturally passes from mother to child. Bonnie started her design business, Cotton Way, in 1990. After a decade of creating dolls, she began designing quilts. It is work that she thoroughly enjoys, and her three daughters have also been bitten by the quilt bug.

Tracy, the oldest daughter, helps Bonnie with Cotton Way. Middle daughter Camille has started her own quilt design company and has co-created a line of fabrics with Bonnie. Youngest daughter Emily is also a quilt designer.

Other Very Important People in Bonnie's life are her husband, two sons, and a growing number of adorable grandchildren. As Bonnie says, "Life is good!"

Visit cottonway.bigcartel.com to see more of Bonnie's quilt patterns and fabrics.

Metric Conversion Chart

Inches x 2.54 = centimeters (cm)			Yards x .9144 = meters (m)		
Inches x 25.4 = millimeters (mm)			Yards x 91.44 = centimeters (cm)		
Inches x .0254 = meters (m)			Centimeters x .3937 = inches (")		
			Meters x 1.0936 = yards (yd)		

Standard Equivalents

$1/8$"	3.2 mm	0.32 cm	$1/8$ yard	11.43 cm	0.11 m
$1/4$"	6.35 mm	0.635 cm	$1/4$ yard	22.86 cm	0.23 m
$3/8$"	9.5 mm	0.95 cm	$3/8$ yard	34.29 cm	0.34 m
$1/2$"	12.7 mm	1.27 cm	$1/2$ yard	45.72 cm	0.46 m
$5/8$"	15.9 mm	1.59 cm	$5/8$ yard	57.15 cm	0.57 m
$3/4$"	19.1 mm	1.91 cm	$3/4$ yard	68.58 cm	0.69 m
$7/8$"	22.2 mm	2.22 cm	$7/8$ yard	80 cm	0.8 m
1 "	25.4 mm	2.54 cm	1 yard	91.44 cm	0.91 m

Production Team: Technical Editor – Lisa Lancaster; Technical Writer – Frances Huddleston; Editorial Writer – Susan Frantz Wiles;

Senior Graphic Artist – Lora Puls; Graphic Artist – Cailen Cochran.

We have made every effort to ensure that these instructions are accurate and complete. We cannot, however, be responsible for human error, typographical mistakes, or variations in individual work.

Copyright © 2016 by Leisure Arts, Inc., 104 Champs Blvd., STE 100, Maumelle, AR 72113-6738. All rights reserved. This publication is protected under federal copyright laws. Reproduction or distribution of this publication or any other Leisure Arts publication, including publications which are out of print, is prohibited unless specifically authorized. This includes, but is not limited to, any form of reproduction or distribution on or through the Internet, including posting, scanning, or e-mail transmission.